'Twas the Night

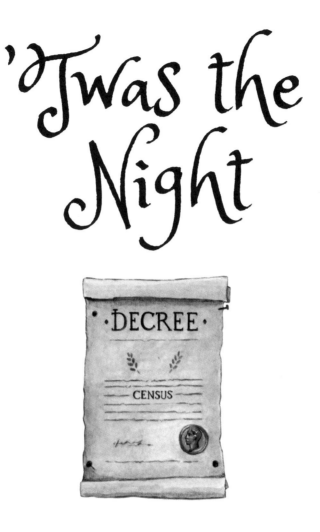

by William Dean
Illustrated by Sarah Lowe

TYNDALE KIDS

Tyndale House Publishers
Carol Stream, Illinois

Visit Tyndale's website for kids at tyndale.com/kids.

Tyndale is a registered trademark of Tyndale House Ministries. The Tyndale Kids logo is a trademark of Tyndale House Ministries.

'Twas the Night

First printing by Tyndale House Publishers in 2023.

Designed by Lindsey Bergsma

Scripture quotations are taken from the (NASB®) New American Standard Bible,® copyright © 1960, 1971, 1977, 1995 by The Lockman Foundation. Used by permission. All rights reserved. www.lockman.org.

For manufacturing information regarding this product, please call 1-855-277-9400.

For information about special discounts for bulk purchases, please contact Tyndale House Publishers at csresponse@tyndale.com, or call 1-855-277-9400.

Library of Congress Cataloging-in-Publication Data

A catalog record for this book is available from the Library of Congress.

ISBN 978-1-4964-7607-4

Printed in the United States of America

29 28 27 26 25 24 23

8   7   6   5   4   3   2

To every little Mary or Joseph,
shepherd or lamb, wise man or angel,
who has ever appeared in a Christmas play:
you have made the season special for me.

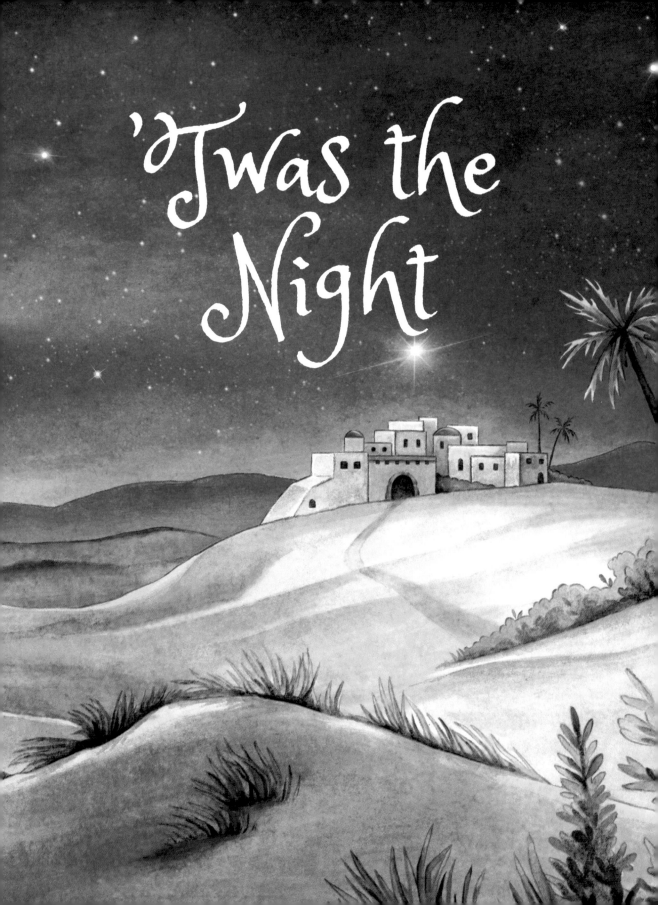

'Twas the Night

'Twas the night before Christmas, and all through the land,
not a creature suspected that God became man.

So hear now the story that tells of God's grace:
long ago was the time, Bethlehem was the place.

People were coming from miles around
to register in this quaint little town.

They had to pay taxes; it was Caesar's decree—
but God had a plan to save you and me.

The town was asleep, the streets were all bare.
No one knew that two travelers soon would be there.

The man was called Joseph, his wife's name was Mary,
plus One yet unborn that God told her to carry.

And when they arrived in the dark of the night,
there was only one place that still had a light.

While Mary sat patting her soft little mound,
Joseph went to the inn, but no room could be found.

"There's a place in the stable," the innkeeper said,
"with plenty of straw for making a bed."

So Mary and Joseph settled down in the stall
as their eyelids grew heavy and started to fall.

All of a sudden, there arose such a clatter,
Joseph woke from his sleep and asked, "What's the matter?"

Her time was upon her; it wouldn't be long,
for the birth of our Savior, so helpless yet strong.

And then it was over, as His cry split the night.
Our darkness was driven away by His light.

The heavens were opened to mark this event,
and glorious angels from the Father were sent
to shepherds attending their flocks in the night,
who didn't expect this incredible sight!

An angel who lit up the sky with his glory
delivered the news of the wonderful story.

"Don't be afraid," the angel proclaimed.
"A Savior is born," is how he explained
the news that he carried from heaven to earth
of God's special plan for this Child's birth.

The night then exploded with angels on high
giving glory to God as they flooded the sky.

"Let's go into town," the old shepherd said,
expressing a thought going round in his head.
"The things we just heard would be something to see."
So he beckoned his friends, and he said, "Follow me."

In a stable, they found, as the angel had said,
an old wooden manger being used for a bed.

The cattle were lowing while He slept on the hay.
The shepherds crept closer to see where He lay,
wrapped, oh so tightly, in swaddling clothes,
so all you could see were His eyes and His nose.

Mary, now resting, was happy to share
all that took place under God's tender care—
How this miracle happened, how the die had been cast,
a virgin with Child, foretold in the past.

She said, "Call Him Jesus. He'll save us from sin."
Then silence befell them as awe settled in.

The shepherds were moved by all they had heard,
so they went on their way, gladly spreading the word.

And as they were leaving, the night echoed again:
"Peace on the earth, good will to all men!"

The angel said to them, "Do not be afraid; for behold, I bring you good news of great joy which will be for all the people; for today in the city of David there has been born for you a Savior, who is Christ the Lord. This will be a sign for you: you will find a baby wrapped in cloths and lying in a manger."

LUKE 2:10-12

ABOUT THE AUTHOR

WILLIAM DEAN realized he loved to write and create when he started inventing scripts and ingenious props for puppet shows that he produced for the enjoyment of his church family. The Christmas productions became his favorites, and over the years, he directed numerous holiday programs for the church and other venues. His first children's book, *'Twas the Night*, was penned in preparation for a program he directed in 2018. William and his wife, Margene, live in the western suburbs of Chicago. They enjoy spending time with friends and family, including their four grown sons, three lovely daughters-in-law, and nine grandchildren.

ABOUT THE ILLUSTRATOR

Having a mother who was a kindergarten and Sunday school teacher, SARAH LOWE grew up on children's books, Bible stories, and crayons. She is now an illustrator of textiles, games, decor, and dozens of book covers. Together with her husband, she created the children's book *The Unshakeable Faith of Gus Mustardseed*. Sarah has three wonderful children whose expressions and shenanigans give her inspiration for her work and draw her nearer to Jesus. She was honored to illustrate this book for William Dean and prays it will bring hope to many. Follow @thelowescreate on Instagram to see what she's working on!